"The Where the HELL is the Alcohol?"

Crazy Cocktail and Devilish Dessert Cookbook

By: Tipsy Tiffany

Acapulco Ass Kicker

Glass:
10 oz./285mL HI-BALL GLASS

Mixers:
1 oz./30mL TEQUILA
1 oz./30mL DARK RUM
5 oz./145mL COCONUT CREAM
ICE CUBES

Garnishes:
Orange or lemon slice

Instructions:
Shake ingredients in a shaker. Do a little dance while you're shaking it! Then strain over ice in a 10 oz. hi-ball glass. Serve with a garnish of orange or lemon wedge.

After Eight....and you're freaking late!

Glass:
2 oz./60mL Fancy Shooter Glass

Mixers:
½ oz./15mL KAHLUA
1/3 oz./10mL CRÈME DE MENTHE
2/3 oz./20mL BAILEY'S IRISH CREAM
2 drops of lemon (optional)

Garnish:
A twist of lemon or orange peel.

Instructions:
Layer ingredients in the given order into a tall Dutch glass or fancy shooter glass. Serve and be merry!

Bloodhound Bitch
....and I'm not talking about the dog

Glass:
5 oz./145 Cocktail Glass

Mixers:
½ oz./15mL DRY VERMOUTH
3-4 dashes of STRAWBERRY LIQUEUR
½ oz./15mL GIN
2-3 STRAWBERRIES (leaves removed)
½ oz./15 mL SWEET VERMOUTH
3-4 ICE CUBES

Garnish:
2-3 strawberries

Instructions:
Blend two-three ice cubes, gin, both types of vermouth, strawberry liqueur and two strawberries. Blend well...put your hand in the air and yell in excitement! Pour into glass over the remaining ice cubes. Garnish with remaining strawberries and serve it sassy.

Bloody Scary Mary

Glass:
10 oz./285mL HI-BALL GLASS

Mixers:

2oz./60mL VODKA (or white rum or tequila)
1 dash WORCESTERSHIRE SAUCE
1/3 oz./10mL LEMON JUICE
2-3 drops of TABASCO SAUCE
TOMATO JUICE
3-4 ICE CUBES
SALT
PEPPER

Instructions:

Pour vodka, sauces, lemon juices, with a sprinkle of salt and pepper. Top it off with tomato juice and ice cubes. Serve with swizzle stick and straws.

Have fun and garnish with a slice of lemon or orange. Be creative.

Blue Bulldog

Glass:
10 oz./285mL HI-BALL GLASS

Mixers:

1 oz./30mL PERNOD
1 teaspoon LEMON JUICE
1 teaspoon BLUE CURACAO
BITTER LEMON (soft drink)
ICE CUBES

Garnish:
Slice of lemon

Instructions:

Pour the mixers over ice in the glass. Top with bitter lemon.
Garnish with the slice of lemon and serve with straws.

Bourbon Banana

Glass:
Brandy balloon

Mixers:
1 oz. BOURBON
1 oz. ORANGE JUICE
1 oz. KAHLUA
1 oz. CREAM
1 BANANA
CRUSHED ICE

Instructions:

Blend the ingredients with ice and serve in a brandy balloon.

Betty Blast

Glass:

5 oz. OLD FASHIONED SPIRIT GLASS

Mixers:

1 oz. GIN
½ oz. AMER PICON
1/3 oz. ORANGE JUICE
1/3 oz. LEMON JUICE
CRUSHED ICE

Instructions:

Blend all the ingredients with ice and pour into glass. Enjoy!

Caribbean Champagne

Glass:
5 oz. Champagne Saucer

Mixers:

4 oz. CHAMPAGNE
1 oz. BACARDI RUM
1 oz. BANANA LIQUEUR
½ oz. ORANGE BITTERS
BANANA SLICE

Instructions:

Stir all the ingredients without ice and pour into a glass.
Garnish with the slice of banana. Now imagine that you're in
the Caribbean.

Cherry Bomb
(Not for your every-day mom!)

Glass:
10 oz. Margarita glass, sugar frosted

Mixers:

1 teaspoon CASTER SUGAR
1 teaspoon GRENADINE CORDIAL
1 oz. VODKA
½ oz. CHERRY BRANDY
7-UP
CRUSHED ICE

Instructions:

Color sugar with grenadine and prepare the glass by sugar-frosting the rim.

Blend the other ingredients over ice and pour into the glass. Top with 7-UP. Add flair by garnished with a flower.

Chasing Chicago

Glass:
5 oz. cocktail glass

Mixers:
1-2 oz. of BRANDY
1 dash ANGOSTURA BITTERS
1 teaspoon COINTREAU
2-3 ICE CUBES
SPARKLING WHITE WINE

Instructions:

Pour the spirits into the glass over ice. Top with white wine and serve. Enjoy!

Chateau

Glass:
6 oz. prism rocks glass

Mixers:
1 oz. COINTREAU
¼ FRESH LIME or LEMON
CRUSHED ICE

Instructions:

Cut lime into pieces and place in glass and extract the juice. Fill the glass with crushed ice and add Cointreau. Stir and enjoy.

Death by Chocolate

Glass:
Champagne saucer

Mixers:
1 oz. BAILEY'S IRISH CREAM
1 oz. CRÈME DE CACAO
1 oz. KAHLUA
3 oz. WHIPPING CREAM
1 oz. TIA MARIA
ICE CUBES
GRATED CHOCOLATE

Instructions:

Shake with ice and pour into the champagne saucer. Garnish with grated chocolate and serve. Find more chocolate and eat that while enjoying your drink.

Ditzy Blonde

Glass:
10 oz. HI-BALL GLASS

Mixers:
2 oz. ADVOCAAT
1 oz. PERNOD
7-UP
CRACKED ICE
1 or 2 MARASCHINO CHERRIES

Instructions:

Fill half the glass with cracked ice and add advocaat and pernod. Top with 7-UP and garnish with a cherry or two. Serve and get ditzy.

D*ck Punch

Glass:
3-4 oz. cocktail glass

Mixers:
 2 oz. CALVADOS
½ oz. DRY VERMOUTH
1 dash of ANGOSTURA BITTERS
ICE CUBES
1 OLIVE
1 strip of LEMON or ORANGE RIND

Instructions:
Mix the ingredients and pour into the glass. Garnish with an
olive and lemon/orange rind.

Easy Erica

Glass:
4 oz. cocktail glass

Ingredients:
1 oz. GIN
1 oz. ORANGE JUICE
1 oz. APRICOT BRANDY
1 oz. CALVADOS
CRACKED ICE
1 APPLE SLICE

Instructions:

Shake all ingredients with ice....shake....shake...shake. Strain the mixture into the glass. Garnish with an apple slice and serve.

East Apron

Glass:
3 oz. fancy martini glass

Ingredients:
1 oz. VODKA
2-3 dashes of WHITE RUM
½ oz. DRY VERMOUTH
½ oz. WHITE VERMOUTH
CRACKED ICE
SLICE OF LIME or LEMON

Instructions:

Mix all ingredients with ice and pour into glass. Serve and enjoy.

F*cking 50

Glass:
5 oz. champagne glass

Instructions:

1 oz. BARCARDI RUM
1 oz. ADVOCAAT
1 oz. ORANGE JUICE
1 oz. CREAM
ICE CUBES
1-2 ORANGE SLICES
1-2 RED CHERRIES

Instructions:
Shake all ingredients with ice and pour into glass. Have fun and garnish with orange slice and red cherries.

Flying Ditch

Glass:
Any glass of your choice

Instructions:

8-10 SMALL LIME CHUNKS
1 teaspoon RAW SUGAR
1 oz. FRANGELICO
1 oz. VODKA
2 oz. CRANBERRY JUICE
ICE CUBES

Instructions:

Place lime and sugar in class. Add the alcohol, ice, and top with cranberry juice. Stir....stir...stir and serve.

Flaming Frankie

Glass:
Any glass of your choice

Mixers:
1 oz. GRANGELICO
½ oz. LIME CORDIAL
SODA WATER
LEMON/LIME SLICE

Stir alcohol and pour over ice. Now top it with soda water.
Garnish with lemon or lime slice.

French 28

Glass:
5 oz. cocktail glass

Mixers:
1 oz. CRÈME DE GRAND MARNIER
1 oz. VODKA
½ oz. TIA MARIA
1 oz. PINEAPPLE JUICE
1 oz. ORANGE JUICE
ICE CUBES
BANANA SLICE
RED CHERRY...or more

Instructions:
Shake time!!!! Shake all the ingredients with ice and pour into glass. Garnish with a banana slice and red cherries.

Genevieve

Glass:
7 oz. HI-BALL GLASS

Mixers:
1 oz. GIN
1 oz. GRAPPA
½ oz. SAMBUCA
½ oz. DRY VERMOUTH
ICE CUBES
OLIVES

Instructions:

Shake all the ingredients and pour over ice. Garnish with
olives.

Geneva Chocolate Cake

Glass:
10 oz. Hurricane glass

Mixers:
1 oz. KAHLUA
1 oz. MALIBU
2 oz. CHOCOLATE SYRUP
1-2 CHOPPED PECANS
2 scoops of VANILLA (or CHOCOLATE) ICE CREAM
CRUSHED ICE

Instructions:
Place the crushed ice into the glass.
Stir everything (you can leave out a little of the chopped pecans-----use as a garnish later) and pour into glass. Now you can garnish with chopped nuts.

Gibson

Glass:
3 oz. cocktail glass

Mixers:
2 oz. GIN
½ oz. DRY VERMOUTH
COCKTAIL ONION
ICE CUBES

Instructions:
Shake....shake....shake. Pour into glass. Add one cocktail onion and enjoy.

Gray Moon

Glass:
3 oz. cocktail glass

Mixers:
1 oz. GALLIANO LIQUEUR
1 oz. WHITE CRÈME DE CACAO
1 oz. FRESH CREAM
YOUR CHOICE OF FRUIT

Instructions:
Blend all the ingredients with ice and pour into glass. Add a
little flair and garnish with your choice of fruit.

Gotcha Stripper

Glass:
3 oz. cocktail glass

Mixers:

1 oz. YELLOW CHARTREUSE
½ oz. APRICOT BRANDY
1 EGG YOLK

Instructions:
Shake over ice and pour into glass.

Hairy Harry

Glass:
10 oz. HI-BALL GLASS

Mixers:

2 oz. VODKA
4 oz. ORANGE JUICE
1 oz. GALLIANO LIQUEUR
ICE CUBES
ORANGE SLICE/WEDGE
2-3 CHERRIES

Instructions:
Mix vodka, orange juice, and ice. Add the Galliano and garnish
how you like with the orange slice and cherries.
Enjoy!

Heartbeat

Glass:
Any 8 oz. glass of your choice.

Mixers:

1 oz. STRAWBERRY LIQUEUR
2 oz. CREAM
½ oz. TIA MARIA
4-5 STRAWBERRIES
½ oz. COINTREAU
CRUSHED ICE

Instructions:

Blend together and pour into glass. Add a strawberry or two as a garnish. Sip and relax.

Honey Bee Hive

Glass:
Any 5 oz. glass

Mixers:

1 oz. BRANDY
1 oz. HONEY
½ oz. GALLIANO LIQUEUR
2 oz. CREAM
½ oz. GRENADINE CORDIAL
CRACKED ICE

Instructions:

Shake time! Shake....shake...shake all the ingredients together.
Pour into glass and garnish how you like.

Horseshoe

Glass:
Any 10 oz. glass

Mixers:
1 oz. DARK RUM
1 EGG YOLK
1 oz. COINTREAU
SPARKLING WHITE WINE
3-4 ICE CUBES

Instructions:
Shake all the ingredients (except the wine). Pour into glass and add the wine. Add a garnish if you like.

Iowa Way

Glass:
Cocktail glass of your choice

Mixers:
1 oz. BOURBON
1 oz. LEMON JUICE
1 oz. BRANDY
2 oz. ORANGE JUICE
ICE CUBES

Instructions:
Mix all ingredients together with ice and pour into glass.
Garnish with a lemon or lime slice. YUMMY!

Irish Lass

Glass:
5 oz. margarita glass

Mixers:

½ oz. MALIBU
2 oz. CREAM
1 oz. STRAWBERRY LIQUEUR
1 teaspoon VANILLA EXTRACT
½ oz. WHITE CRÈME DE CACAO
1 scoop of VANILLA ICE CREAM

Instructions:
Mix all ingredients until smooth and pour into the glass. Serve
and make again.

Jelly Belly

Glass:
4-5 oz. cocktail glass

Mixers:

2 oz. cream
½ oz. GALLIANO LIQUEUR
1 oz. ANISETTE LIQUEUR
ICE CUBES
ORANGE OR LEMON SLICE

Instructions:
Mix all ingredients together and pour over ice. Feel free to
garnish with an orange or lemon slice.

Killing Kimmy

Glass:
10 oz. glass of your choice

Mixers:
1 oz. SOUTHERN COMFORT
½ oz. SUGAR SYRUP
1 oz. BAILEYS IRISH CREAM
3-4 STRAWBERRIES
2 oz. MILK
CRUSHED ICE

Instructions:
Mix all the ingredients together and pour into the glass. Serve with strawberries.

Knockout!

Glass:
10 oz. glass of your choice

Mixers:

1 oz. SCOTCH WHISKY
1 EGG YOLK
½ oz. SUGAR SYRUP
CRACKED ICE
SPARKLING WHITE WINE
1 ORANGE or LEMON RIND

Instructions:
Blend all the ingredients except the wine. Pour the mixture into the glass. Top the drink with wine and serve with an orange or lemon rind for garnish.

Lucy Love

Glass:
5-6 oz. glass of your choice

Mixers:

1 oz. VODKA
½ oz. of LEMON JUICE
1 oz. STRAWBERRY LIQUEUR
½ oz. GRENADINE CORDIAL
5-6 STRAWBERRIES
CRACKED ICE
MORE STRAWBERRIES for garnish

Instructions:
Mix all the ingredients with ice and pour into the glass. Serve
with the extra strawberries.

Morning Glory

Glass:
5 oz. of your choice

Mixers:

1oz. SCOTCH
1 oz. BRANDY
1 teaspoon PERNOD
1 teaspoon WHITE CURACAO
2 dashes ANGOSTURA BITTERS
SODA WATER
ICE CUBES
ORANGE RIND or LEMON WEDGE

Instructions:
Shake all ingredients except soda water with ice. Pour the mixture into the glass. Top with soda water and garnish with orange twist or lemon wedge.

Moscow Mule

Glass:
10 oz. HI-BALL GLASS

Mixers:

1 oz. VODKA
½ oz. LIME CORDIAL
GINGER BEER
ICE CUBES
LEMON SLICE
1 MINT SPRIG (optional)

Instructions:
Build in glass over ice. Garnish with a slice of lemon and mint.
Add a straw and enjoy.

McKinley

Glass:
3 oz. cocktail glass

Mixers:

½ oz. PEAR BRANDY
1 dash of ORANGE BITTERS
½ oz. APRICOT BRANDY
½ oz. SWEET VERMOUTH
CRACKED ICE
1-2 MARASCHINO CHERRIES

Instructions:
Shake it time! Shake all the ingredients together and pour into a glass. Garnish with cherries and serve.

Naughty Nipple

Glass:
8 oz. glass of your choice

Mixers:

1 oz. TIA MARIA
½ BANANA
½ oz. JAMAICAN RUM
2 oz. ORANGE JUICE
2 oz. PINEAPPLE JUICE
CRACKED ICE
1-2 PINEAPPLE WEDGES
1-2 CHERRIES

Instructions:
Blend all the ingredients until smooth and pour into the glass.
Garnish with pineapple wedges and cherries. Ready to serve!

New York....New York!

Glass:
A fancy cocktail glass....about 3 oz.

Mixers:

½ oz. GIN
1 dash of COINTREAU
1 ½ oz. DRY VERMOUTH
CRACKED ICE
½ oz. SWEET CHERRY
ORANGE or LEMON RIND

Instructions:
Stir all the ingredients together. Pour into a glass, add the
orange or lemon rind, and enjoy!

Nutty Ned

Glass:
2-3 oz. glass of your choice

Mixers:

½ oz. KAHLUA
½ oz. CRÈME DE MENTHE
½ oz. FRANGELICO

Instructions:
Layer in order....and drink.

Naughty Irish

Glass:
Irish coffee glass

Mixers:

1 oz. FRANGELICO
1 oz. BAILEY'S IRISH CREAM
2 oz. CREAM
CHOCOLATE FLAKES

Instructions:
Shake all the ingredients together and pour into a glass.
Garnish with chocolate flakes and serve.

Out of the Office

Glass:
Cocktail or champagne glass

Mixers:

3 oz. BRANDY
1 oz. SWEET VERMOUTH
CRACKED ICE
3-4 MARASCHINO CHERRIES

Instructions:
Mix all the ingredients together and pour into a glass. Add the cherries and enjoy!

Orgasm

Glass:
7 oz. spirit glass.....or whatever glass you choose to drink your
"orgasm" from.

Mixers:

1 oz. BAILEY'S IRISH CREAM
1 oz. COINTREAU
ICE CUBES
STRAWBERRIES OR CHERRIES

Instructions:
Build over ice....garnish with strawberries or cherries.

Prairie Moose

Glass:
3 oz. cocktail glass

Mixers:

1 oz. BRANDY
SALT and PEPPER
1 dash of WORCESTERSHIRE SAUCE
1 dash of TABASCO SAUCE
1 EGG YOLK

Instructions:
Build the ingredients in order and enjoy.

Happy Ass Peppermint Schnapps Cake

Cake:
1 package of Devil's Food cake mix
1 large package of instant chocolate pudding
4 eggs
½ cup of water
½ cup of oil
½ cup of Peppermint Schnapps
½ cup of chopped walnuts (optional)
½ cup of chocolate chips (optional)

Glaze:
½ cup of melted butter
¼ cup of water
1 cup of white sugar
½ cup of Peppermint Schnapps

Frosting (option 1):
1 cup of heavy cream (very cold)
1/3 cup of powdered sugar
2 tsp. of peppermint schnapps
Mix all the ingredients together...you can use a stand mixer.
Beat on high, hopefully soft peaks will form.
This should take about 3 minutes.

Frosting (option 2):
4 ounces of unsalted butter
4 ounces of cream cheese (softened)
2 cups of powdered sugar
Cap of vanilla or peppermint schnapps
Mix the butter & cream cheese together with an electric mixer.
Add powdered sugar a bit at a time.
Add the vanilla/peppermint schnapps

Stir until creamy

Create the cake mixture.
If you are using nuts, place them in the bottom of a sprayed
Bundt cake pan.
Pour the mixture over the nuts.
Bake at 325 degrees for an hour.
When the hour is up, remove the cake from the oven. Keep the
pan upside down.
Now to the glaze...in a saucepan, mix all the ingredients (except
for the Peppermint Schnapps) & boil for about 5 minutes.
Remove the glaze mixture from the stove & cool a few minutes.
Stir in the Peppermint Schnapps into the glaze mixture.
With the cake still upside down, poke a few holes on the top
with a steak knife. You can use a fork to do this if you wish.
Pour the glaze over top and let it cool...about an hour.

Create frosting mixture.
Remove the cake from the pan & put it on a decorative plate.
Spread the frosting mixture on top.
Crush some peppermint candy (like Candy Canes) & sprinkle
on top.

After I create this beyond delicious dessert, I gently wrap it in
saran wrap & place in the freezer to chill.
This cake is excellent cold.
DO NOT OPERATE HEAVY MACHINERY OR POWER TOOLS
AFTER EATING A PIECE!

AWESOME CAKE!

Big Butt Cake Batter Fudge

2 cups of white or yellow cake mix
2 cups of powdered sugar
1 stick of butter (I cut this into 5 or 6 pieces)
¼ cup of milk
½ cup of white chocolate chips
About ½ cup of sprinkles...or more!

In a microwave safe bowl stir the cake mix & powdered sugar.
Add butter and milk (you don't need to stir)
Microwave on high for 2 minutes.
Take out of the microwave & stir.
Once the fudge mixture is blended, add the white chips.
Stir some more
Stir in about half of your sprinkles...the mixture needs a little pizzazz.
Spread the mixture in a greased pan. I use an 8 x 8 sprayed/greased pan.
Add the remaining sprinkles to the top & pat down a little.
Refrigerate until it's chilled.
Cut into small squares.
ENJOY!

Bacon Brittle

1 ½ cups of sugar
½ cup of light corn syrup
¾ cup of water (cold)
1 lb. or more of cooked and crumbled bacon (I use crispy bacon)
1 tsp. of baking soda
Pinch of salt
Cap of vanilla

Butter a 9 x 13 baking sheet.
Put that aside.

Mix the sugar, corn syrup, water, and salt in a saucepan.
Bring to a boil over medium-heat & stir.
Cook until it gets to about 238 degrees on a candy thermometer.
Add the bacon.
Stir...be careful not to burn.
Add the vanilla and baking soda.
Stir carefully.
Pour the mixture onto the 9 x 13 pan.
Spread it evenly on the pan and let it cool.

When it's cooled...take a hammer and break it!

Purple Octopus Chocolate Soup

1 cup of milk
½ cup of heavy whipping cream
2 tablespoons unsweetened cocoa powder
2 tablespoons white sugar
Cap of vanilla
Small pinch of ground cinnamon (1/4 teaspoon)

Heat cream and milk (except 3 teaspoons) in a saucepan.
DO NOT BOIL

In a small bowl mix the cocoa, sugar, vanilla, cinnamon and the
3 tablespoons of the cream and milk mixture.
Mix everything together and blend well.
Pour into a bowl of your choice & add some marshmallows.
For extra "pizzazz" I mix in a few squares of dark chocolate.

Grilled Candy Bars

16 teaspoons of marshmallow fluff
8 small tortillas (I use flour)
8 candy bars of your choice
8 teaspoons of unsalted melted butter
Pinches of sugar
Pinches of brown sugar (optional)

Spread 2 teaspoons of marshmallow fluff on each tortilla.
Place a candy bar in the center.
Wrap the tortilla around the candy bar, seal it entirely with marshmallow fluff.
Lightly brush the outside of the tortillas with melted butter.
Sprinkle lightly with sugar...either white, brown or both.
Wrap each tortilla in aluminum foil.
Place the tortilla aluminum packages on a cookie sheet.
Place in the oven for a few minutes.
Cool for about 3 or 4 minutes before unwrapping foil.

If using a grill: grill these over medium heat for about 5 minutes on each side.

Magic Mitch's Maple Bacon Popcorn

About 10 cups of popped popcorn
One pound of cooked bacon (or more)—crumbled
A few tablespoons of bacon drippings
¾ cup of maple syrup
1 teaspoon of pepper
Pinch or two of salt

Preheat oven to 350 degrees.
Line a cookie sheet with parchment paper.
In a large bowl mix the popcorn and bacon together.
In a different bowl mix the bacon drippings, maple syrup, black pepper & salt together.
Pour the maple syrup mixture over the popcorn & bacon.
Toss it to coat.
Spread the popcorn in a single layer on the pan.
Bake for about 10 to 13 minutes.
Stir it occasionally.

Run Through the Streets Naked Fuzzy Navel Cake

Cake:
1 box of yellow cake mix (18 ounce)
½ cup of vegetable oil
1 package of vanilla instant pudding mix
4 eggs
¾ peach schnapps
½ cup of orange juice
½ teaspoon of orange extract

Glaze:
4 tablespoons of peach schnapps
2 tablespoons of orange juice
1 cup of powdered sugar

Mix all the cake ingredients together.
Pour into a greased Bundt pan.
Bake at 350 degrees for 45 to 50 minutes.
While the cake is baking, create the glaze.
Mix all the ingredients together for the glaze with a mixer.
While the cake is still warm, poke holes in the cake.
I use a knife.
Pour the glaze over the cake.
Allow the cake to cool for at least 2 hours.
Remove & enjoy!

If you wish to add a frosting mixture to the top of the cake,
please see below.
Frosting:
4 ounces of unsalted butter
4 ounces of cream cheese (softened)
2 cups of powdered sugar
Cap of vanilla or peach schnapps
Mix the butter & cream cheese together with an electric mixer.
Add powdered sugar a bit at a time.
Add the vanilla/peach schnapps
Stir until creamy

OR...
You can double the glaze recipe & pour over the top of the cake
after you remove it from the pan.

Chocolate Dream Cream Fudge

¾ cup of butter
3 cups of sugar
2/3 cup of evaporated milk
1 cup of nuts (optional)
Cap full of vanilla
1 (12 oz.) pkg. of real chocolate chips
1 (7 oz.) jar of marshmallow crème

In a saucepan combine butter, 3 cups of sugar & evaporated milk.
Cook to a full boil for about 5 minutes over medium heat.
Remove from stove and add chocolate chips, vanilla and marshmallow crème.
If you would like to add a bit of dark chocolate…go for it!

Sassy Ass Nut Roll Bars

2 T of butter
15 oz. of sweetened condensed milk
2 cups of miniature marshmallows
12 oz. pkg. peanut butter chips
16 oz. jar dry roasted peanuts

If you would like to "mix 'n match" peanuts with cashews, almonds, or a nut of your choice, please do so.

Spread ½ jar of peanuts on the bottom of a greased 9 x 13 inch pan. Melt butter, peanut butter chips and sweetened condensed milk on low heat.
Add marshmallows.
Spread the gooey mixture over peanuts and top with remaining peanuts.
If you would like to add a sprinkle of milk chocolate chips on top, go for it.
You can't go wrong with chocolate!

Jalapeno Chocolate Cake

Cake mixture:
1 cup of chocolate chips (melted & cooled)
¾ cup of butter
1 ¼ cups of sugar
Cap of vanilla
3 eggs
2 cups of flour
1 tablespoon of cinnamon
2 teaspoons of baking soda or baking powder
Pinch of salt
1 cup of milk
2 tablespoons of canned jalapenos (chopped)
Preheat oven to 350 degrees
Spray or grease two 9 inch round baking pans.

Mix all the cake ingredients together.
Blend well.
Bake for 30 to 35 minutes or until a wooden inserted toothpick comes out clean.
Cool in pans for about 20 minutes.
Transfer to wire racks to finish cooling.
Frosting:
3- 3 ¼ cups of powdered sugar
1/3 cup of milk
½ cup of butter (softened)
A cap or two of vanilla
3 teaspoons of cocoa powder
Pinch of salt
1 ½ to 2 cups of almonds
For the frosting, beat all the ingredients together until baby butt smooth.
Frost the cake.
Decorate the side with almonds!

Olive Oil & Honey Ice Cream

Ingredients:
3 egg yolks (already whisked)
2 cups of whole milk
1 cup of cream
½ cup of sugar
½ cup of olive oil
¼ cup of honey
¾ teaspoon of salt
Cap of vanilla

Do not boil...but heat the milk, cream, sugar, honey & salt on low heat.
Remove from heat.
Drizzle 2 cups of the mixture into a bowl with the egg yolks.
Whisk constantly!
Pour the egg yolk mixture back into the saucepan.
Whisk constantly! ☺

Whisk this on low heat...for about 5 to 10 minutes.
The mixture should be thickening.
Remove from the heat.
Whisk in olive oil & vanilla until everything is nicely combined.
Let this cool to room temperature.
Cover and refrigerate for at least 4 hours or overnight.
Now prepare your ice cream maker according to the manufacturers directions.
Take the mixture out of the freezer & whisk it quick before pouring it into the ice cream maker.
The mixture should take about 25 minutes to look ice cream like.
Pour the ice cream into a freezer safe container.

Freeze this bad boy ice cream for at least 4 hours before serving.
For an extra "cha-cha" factor...you can drizzle a little olive oil on top before serving.
Delicious!
P.S. I would only use the best kind of olive oil for this.

Rich Bitch Peanut Butter Popcorn

½ cup of unpopped popcorn or 6 cups of popped popcorn
(about 2 bags of microwavable popcorn)
1 ½ cups of dry roasted peanuts
1 cup of sugar
½ cup of honey
½ cup of corn syrup
1 cup of peanut butter (I like creamy, but you can use crunchy)
Cap of vanilla
A handful of chocolate chips (optional)
Crushed up peanut butter cups (optional)

Pop the corn and remove any unpopped kernels.
Place the popcorn in a large bowl.
In a saucepan combine sugar, honey & corn syrup. Bring the
mixture to a boil, stirring constantly.
Don't boil for a long period of time.
Remove from heat & stir in peanut butter and vanilla.
Pour this mixture over the popcorn and stir to coat.
If you want...stir in chocolate chips & peanut butter cups.
Serve warm or at room temperature.

Fat Fred's Applesauce & Coffee Cake

1 cup applesauce
½ cup of butter (soft)
1 cup of sugar
1 tsp. of soda
1 ½ cup of flour
Dash or two of cinnamon
½ tsp. of nutmeg
½ cup of nuts of your choice

FROSTING:
1 cup of powdered sugar
2 T of butter
Cap of vanilla
Hot coffee (use enough to make the right consistency to spread on the cake.)

Heat the first 3 ingredients until well blended. Add the soda.
Stir everything well.
Let the mixture cool.
Add the next four ingredients; flour, cinnamon, nutmeg & nuts.
Pour into a 9 x 13 inch pan.
Bake for 350 degrees for 30 minutes.
Cool.
Frost and enjoy!

Quirky Cupcakes

One package of cake mix (any flavor)
8 oz. of cream cheese (soft)
1/3 cup of sugar
One egg
Pinch of salt
Cap of vanilla
Cherry pie filling (optional)

Make the cake mix according to directions.
For a "twist" you could skip the oil & eggs on the cake mix directions and substitute it for a small can of pumpkin pie filling or a can of soda.
Pour the cake mixture into cupcake pans that are lined with cupcake liners.
Next, mix the sugar, egg & cream cheese together.
Drop a spoonful of the cream cheese mixture onto each cupcake.
Bake at 350 degrees for 20 minutes.
Add a spoonful or two of cherry pie filling on top, if desired.

Scary Terry Brownies

1 cup of sugar
1 stick of butter
4 eggs
1 can of chocolate syrup
1 cup of flour (plus 2 tbsp.)
Cap of vanilla
Nuts of your choice (if desired)

Frosting:
1 ½ cups of sugar
6 tbsp. of milk
6 tbsp. of butter
Chocolate chips (your choice)

Brownies: Melt butter and mix all the Brownie ingredients together. Spread the mixture on a 10 x 15 jelly roll pan. Bake at 325 degrees until done.
Test it with a toothpick.

Frosting: Bring the frosting ingredients to a boil. Let it boil for about a minute. Remove from the stove and add ½ cup of chocolate chips (part milk chocolate, part semi-sweet) ...for an added touch you can put in a few butterscotch chips.

German Sauerkraut Cupcakes

2/3 cup of butter
1 1/3 cups of white sugar
3 eggs
Cap of vanilla
½ cup of unsweetened cocoa powder
2 ¼ cups of flour
1 teaspoon of baking powder
¾ teaspoon baking soda
Small pinch of salt
1 ¼ cups of water
2/3 cup of sauerkraut (drained & chopped)

Preheat over to 350 degrees.
Mix all ingredients together until well blended.
Pour cake mixture into cupcake liners.
Bake at 350 degrees for about 30 minutes.
Keep an eye on the cupcakes...poke a wooden toothpick & see
if it comes out clean.
Frost with your favorite frosting.

Red's Killer Granola

4 cups of uncooked oatmeal
½ cup of wheat germ
1 cup of slivered almonds
1 cup of sunflower seeds
1 cup of coconut
½ cup of honey
½ cup of brown sugar
¾ cup of vegetable oil
Cap of vanilla
Dash of cinnamon
Tiny pinch of salt (about ½ teaspoon)
1 cup of raisins
½ cup or so of dried cranberries (optional)
½ or a handful of chocolate chips (optional)

Combine all the ingredients (except raisins & cranberries & chocolate chips).
Blend the ingredients well.
Spread the mixture of a baking sheet (I use a shallow one).
Bake at 350 degrees for 25 to 30 minutes.
Stir in raisins (and cranberries and chocolate chips- if you're using them)

Pink Raccoon Popcorn

4 quarts of popped popcorn
8 tbsp. of Strawberry Jello (dry)
3 cups of miniature marshmallows
4 tbsp. of butter
Red food coloring

Melt butter over low heat and stir in marshmallows.
Make sure the marshmallows are soft and not melted.
Add the Jello to the butter and marshmallows.
Stir until the mixture is a nice pink color.
Pour over popcorn and stir until all the popcorn is coated.

Brownies Fit for a Queen

2 cups of sugar
1 cup of butter (soften)
4 eggs
Cap of vanilla
1 ½ cups of flour
Pinch of salt
¼ cup of cocoa
1 cup of chopped nuts of your choice
½ cup or more of milk chocolate chips (or semi sweet)
Chocolate frosting

Mix sugar, butter, eggs and vanilla. Stir in flour and salt. Add
cocoa and nuts. Pour into a greased 9 x 13 pan.
Bake at 350 degrees for 25 minutes.
Frost with chocolate frosting.

Holy Cow I am Late Cookies

1 cake mix (any flavor)
1 egg
4 oz. of cool whip
Powdered sugar (use later...before baking)

Mix the ingredients together.
The dough will be stiff.
Form into balls & roll into powdered sugar.
Bake for 7 to 10 minutes at 350 degrees.
For extra sweetness....spread your favorite frosting on top.

Crazy Next Door Lady Coconut Macaroons
(it cooks faster than you can say it)

1 package of white cake mix
1 (14 oz.) package of flaked coconut
2 cups of vanilla ice cream

Mix everything together well.
Drop by teaspoons on well greased cookie sheet.
Bake at 300 degrees for 20 minutes.
Please do not brown.

BELIEVE IN YOURSELF!

The Bride & Groom are Horny Wedding Cakes

2 cups of flour
1 cup of butter
½ cup of powdered sugar
½ cup of coconut
Cap of vanilla
Pinch of salt
Mix all the ingredients together.
Make sure they are well blended.
Form into small balls & do not flatten.
Bake in oven at 350 degrees until light brown.
Roll in powdered sugar.
Enjoy!

"I Love You Day" Pie

1 unbaked 9 inch pie shell (deep-dish)
2 large eggs
½ cup of flour
½ cup of sugar
½ cup of brown sugar
¾ cup of butter (softened)
1 cup of semi-sweetened chocolate chips
1 cup of chopped nuts (your choice)
Ice cream (optional)

Preheat oven to 325 degrees.
Beat eggs...add flour, sugars, butter, chocolate chips & nuts.
Spoon this mixture into pie shell.
Bake for 55 to 60 minutes.
Cool on wire rack.
Serve with ice cream.
For an extra pizzazz...break up a dark chocolate candy bar & mix into the ingredients before baking.

I've Gone Bananas Cookies

1 ½ cup of sugar
¾ cup of butter
2 eggs
1 cup of mashed banana
Pinch of salt
1 tsp. of baking soda
1 tsp. of baking powder
2 ½ cups of flour (more if needed)
½ cups of chopped nuts (your choice)

Frosting:
1/3 cup of softened butter
Cap of vanilla
2 cups of powdered sugar
2 tablespoons of milk

Mix all the cookie ingredients together.
Drop by spoonfuls on greased cookie sheet.
Bake at 350 degrees for 10 to 12 minutes.
Top the cookies with frosting (or frosting of your choice)

Pep In My Step Cake

1 package of yellow cake mix
1 package of instant pudding (vanilla or lemon)
1 cup of oil
4 eggs
¾ cup of orange juice
¼ cup of vodka
¼ cup of Galliano

Mix all the ingredients together.
Beat together for a couple of minutes.
Bake in a Bundt pan at 350 degrees for 45 to 50 minutes.
Let it cool & remove cake from pan.
Sprinkle with powdered sugar or spread on your favorite frosting (cream cheese frosting works well)

Campfire Brownies

1 cup of butter
2 2/3 cups of sugar
1 cup of flour
Pinch of salt
Cap of vanilla
Handful of chocolate chips
4 eggs
1 ½ tsp. baking powder
1 ½ cups of oatmeal

Mix all the ingredients well. Pour into a 9 x 13 pan. Bake at 350 degrees for 20-25 minutes.
If you would like to spread chocolate frosting on top...go for it!

Jumping Jimmy's Popcorn

4 quarts of popcorn (popped)
That's about ¾ to 1 cup of unpopped kernels
1/3 cup of water
1 cup of butter
1 cup of sugar
Food coloring (optional)
On medium heat combine butter, sugar, water and food coloring.
Stir the mixture constantly.
Pour the mixture over popped popcorn.
Put the popcorn on a cookie sheet (I use a shallow one).
Bake at 300 degrees for 15 minutes.
Stir every few minutes (about 5).
Let it cool.

Cha-Cha Carmel Bars

1 1/3 cup of flour
1 ½ cup of quick oatmeal
1 cup of brown sugar
¾ tsp. of baking soda
Pinch of salt
1 cup of butter (soften)
1 cup of walnuts
1 cup of chocolate chips (semi-sweet or milk)
1 cup of caramel topping

Mix the flour, oatmeal, sugar, baking soda, salt and butter together. Pat 2/3 of the mixture into a greased cake pan. Bake for 10 minutes at 350 degrees.
Remove from the oven. Add nuts, chocolate chips & caramel. Dot the remaining bar mixture on top.
Bake for 20 minutes. Keep an eye on the bars while baking.

Kizzy's Dump Cake

2 cans of sliced peaches (undrained)
1 package of butter pecan cake mix
1 stick of melted butter
1 cup of coconut
1 cup of pecans (chopped)

Layer the first 5 ingredients in order in a 13 x 9 inch pan.
Resist the urge to stir. If you would like to sprinkle a few
chocolate chips on top...go for it.
Bake at 325 degrees for 55 to 60 minutes.
Top with whipped cream or ice cream.

Rocco's Reese Candy Cubes

1 ½ lb. powdered sugar
2 cubes of butter (melted)
Cap of vanilla
2 cups of peanut butter
1 package of chocolate chips

Mix melted butter and powdered sugar. Add vanilla and peanut butter. Blend everything together well.
Flatten mixture to 1 inch thick on a cookie sheet.
Melt chocolate chips in a double boiler and spread a thin layer on the peanut butter mixture. Cook and cut into squares.
If you would like to experiment with the chocolate by adding some butterscotch chips, dark chocolate...go for it!

Ecstasy English Toffee

2 cups of sugar
1 pound of butter
½ cup of white syrup

For later use: 1 pound of chocolate bars.
Pecans or almonds (optional)

Cook the ingredients until the hard stage (295 degrees).
Pour into a greased cookie sheet.
When set, melt 1 pound of chocolate bars.
Spread over top.
Sprinkle with chopped pecans or almonds...or both!
Cut immediately.

Did Someone say, "Chocolate Candy-Bars?"

Crust:
1 ½ cups of flour
¼ cup of sugar
½ cup of butter
Mix flour, sugar, and butter together. Press the mixture into a 7 x 11 inch pan. Bake at 375 degrees for 12 to 15 minutes.

Filling:
1/3 cup of butter
¾ cup of sugar
½ cup of chocolate chips
¼ cup of milk
Cap of vanilla
1 cup of oatmeal
Nuts & coconuts are optional
Melt butter, sugar, chocolate chips & milk. Bring that to a boil and stir constantly.
Remove that from the heat and add vanilla, oatmeal and nuts.
Spread this over warm crust.
Press another ½ cup of chocolate chips (or more) and coconut on top.

Grandpa Ed's German Sugar Popcorn

¼ cup of popcorn
¼ cup of sugar
1 tbsp. of butter
Flavored shortening

Melt shortening in a 1 quart saucepan on high.
Add the popcorn.
When the popcorn starts popping add the sugar and place the
lid on.
Shake the pan to mix sugar.
Shake....shake....and shake some more to keep from burning.
P.S. I have a feeling my Grandfather added a lot more sugar to
his concoctions.

Tornado Turtle Cake

1 box of German chocolate cake mix
½ cup of evaporated milk
1 cup of chocolate chips (or more)
1 (14 oz.) bag of caramels
¾ cup of butter
2 cups of nuts of your choice (chopped)

Prepare the cake using the package directions.
Pour ½ of the batter into a greased 9 x 13 inch pan.
Bake at 350 degrees for 15 minutes.
Melt caramels with butter and milk over low heat in a saucepan.
Stir this constantly.
Pour over this over the cake.
Sprinkle with 1 cup of nuts & chocolate chips.
Pour the remaining batter over the filling.
Sprinkle with remaining nuts & feel free to toss a handful of chocolate chips on top (if you desire.)

Bake this bad boy cake for 20 minutes or a touch longer if needed.

Vivian's Vanilla Wafers

½ cup of butter
¼ cup of sugar
1 large egg
Cap or two of vanilla
¾ cup of flour

Beat butter, sugar, egg & vanilla until well blended.
Add the flour and mix until the dough is smooth.
Drop by teaspoon on a cookie sheet, about an inch apart.
Bake for 350 degrees for 10 to 12 minutes.

Outstanding Oatmeal Sugar Cookies

1 cup of sugar
1 cup of shortening
Pinch of salt
1 tsp. of baking soda
Cap of vanilla
1 ½ cup of flour
1 cup of brown sugar
2 eggs
½ tsp. of baking powder
½ tsp. of cinnamon
3 cups of oatmeal

Mix all the ingredients together.
Form into little balls & roll in sugar.
Hum while you do this or sing a little tune.
Bake at 350 degrees on greased cookie sheets.

Roses in the Snow Cake

1 small angel food cake
1 cup of powdered sugar
1 can of cherry pie filling
8 oz. of cream cheese
1 large container of whipped cream (like Cool Whip)

Beat cream cheese, sugar and whipped cream together until creamy.
Tear the angel food cake apart into small pieces.
Put a layer of the cake into a pan.
Add a layer of the cream cheese mixture and another layer of cake.
Pour the cream cheese mixture on again.
Pour pie filling on top and refrigerate.

P-P-P-Peppermint Patties!

1 cup of oleo
2 cups of sugar
4 eggs
6 T of cocoa
Dash of salt
1 1/3 cups of flour
Cap of vanilla

Filling:
2 T of oleo
3 cups of powered sugar
1 ½ caps of peppermint flavor
Milk

Cream oleo & sugar. Mix well. Add eggs.
Beat the oleo, sugar and eggs together until it's light.
Mix in cocoa, salt & flour.
Mix in vanilla.
Spread in a greased cookie sheet.
Bake at 325 degrees for 25 minutes.

Filling:
Melt oleo and add sugar, peppermint flavoring & enough milk
to mix smooth. Try and get light consistency for spreading.
Spread over cooled brownies.
Put in freezer to set.
Then frost with at least 6 ounces of chocolate chips and 6
tablespoons of oleo melted together.
If you would like to have more frosting....go for it!

Hot Lava Chocolate

2 squares of unsweetened chocolate
½ cup of sugar
1 tablespoon of cornstarch
2 cups of black coffee
1 tablespoon of cinnamon
1 piece of vanilla bean
Pinch of salt
3 cups of hot milk

Melt chocolate with little water over double boiler over low flame. Add sugar & cornstarch mixed together.
Stir in the coffee until the mixture is smooth.
Simmer for about 5 minutes.
Add the cinnamon, vanilla bean & hot milk.
Cook for 30 minutes.
Whip the chocolate to a froth.
Remove the vanilla bean and serve.

Awesome Possum Orange Puffs

½ pound of flour
2 tablespoons of butter
Pinch of salt (about ½ teaspoon)
2 tablespoons of sugar
Juice from 2 oranges
Cold water (if needed)
Fat/butter/etc. for frying
Powdered sugar

Mix all the ingredients into a smooth dough.
Roll out as thin as possible.
Cut into any shape you like.
Fry the dough in fat/butter
Drain, set aside and powder with sugar.

Magic Lamp Coconut & Almond Candy

2 cups of sugar
1 cup of hot milk
1 cup of almonds (chopped)
1 small coconut (grated)
6 egg yolks

Mix sugar & hot milk in a saucepan on stove to a boiling point.
Add almonds (stir constantly)
Let the mixture thicken, but don't let it reach the soft-ball stage.
Add coconut and egg yolks.
Cook gently & stir until mixture is ready to cream.
Let it stand overnight and mold next day.

Holy Sh*t Santa Eggnog

1 part honey
3 parts white rum
1 part lemon or lime juice

Shake well with cracked ice & serve in cocktail glasses.

Yes to Sex Caramels

1 can of sweetened condensed milk
1 ½ cups of corn syrup
2 cups of white sugar
Cap full of vanilla
¼ lb. of butter

In a large saucepan combine milk, syrup, butter & sugar
together.
Bring that to a boil over medium heat for 20 minutes.
Remove the mixture from the heat 7 add vanilla.
Pour into 8 X 8 inch pan.
Chill!
When chilled, turn it onto a cutting board & cut into small
pieces.
You can wrap each piece in plastic wrap.

Billion Dollar Cheese Fudge

1 cup of butter (soft)
8 ounces of pasteurized processed cheese (cut into squares)...Velveeta cheese works well.
1 ½ cups of powdered sugar
½ cup of cocoa (unsweetened)
½ cup of dry milk (can use non-fat)
A few caps of vanilla
Handful of chocolate chips
2 cups of chopped pecans/walnuts/cashews (or mix and match)
Caramel sauce (optional)

In a saucepan over medium heat melt the butter, chocolate chips and cheese.
Stir!
Remove from heat when it's melted.
Add the powdered sugar, dry milk, vanilla & nuts.
Stir!
Pour into a 9x9 pan.
Sometimes I drizzle a little caramel sauce over top of extra zing.
Chill!
Cut into squares.

Sexy Sugar Walnuts

1 cup of sugar
¼ cup of evaporated milk
2 tsp. of water
Dash of cinnamon
1 ½ cups of walnuts (whole halves)
Cap of vanilla
Food coloring of your choice
For extra zip...you can add different nuts to the mixture.

Mix the sugar, milk, water & cinnamon in a saucepan & cook
until soft ball stage.
Add vanilla & nuts.
Add food coloring.
On wax paper spread the nut mixture by spoonful.

Eggnog Toffee Candy Bar Popcorn

About 8 cups or so of popped popcorn (I use kettle corn)
1 package of Eggnog candy melts
About 1 cup of toffee candy bars (crushed, chopped, broken)
A candy bar or two of your choice (I use Kit Kats)
Put waxed paper onto a large cookie sheet.
In a bowl, melt the candy melts according to package directions.
In a large bowl mix the popcorn and candy bars.
Add the candy melts over the popcorn mixture. Gently stir.
Spread the popcorn over wax paper on the cookie sheet.
Sprinkle the toffee candy bars over top.
Let the popcorn sit about 30 minutes.
Break into pieces after the popcorn is set.
Store in an airtight container.

Fire Rocket Candy

1 cup of powdered sugar
3 ¾ cups of white sugar
1 ½ cups of light corn syrup
1 cup of water
Cinnamon oil (at least 2 teaspoons)
Red food coloring
Candy thermometer

Line a cookie sheet with aluminum foil, roll the edges up.
Sprinkle the foil with powdered sugar...I use quite a bit.
In a saucepan combine the white sugar, water & corn starch.
Heat this between medium & high heat.
Stir this constantly while the sugar dissolves.
Stop stirring and boil this until a candy thermometer reads 300 to 310 degrees F.
149 to 154 degrees C.
Remove from the heat.

Stir in the cinnamon oil and food coloring.
Pour onto the foil.
Let it cool & harden.

Break into pieces and enjoy!
Store in an airtight container.

Special Note: You can vary the flavors by substituting lemon, strawberry, grape, orange or other flavors.

Razzle Dazzle Cherry Cobbler

1 can of cherry pie filling (or a flavor of your choice)
1 cup of sugar
1 cup of flour
2/3 cup of milk
1 tbsp. of melted butter
2 tsp. of baking powder
Cap of vanilla
Pinch of salt

Spread the pie filling in an 8 x 10 pan.
Mix the rest of the ingredients and spread on top of the pie mixture.
Bake at 350 degrees for 20 to 30 minutes.
Serve with ice cream or whipped topping.

Penguin Walk Pretzel Fudge

2 cups of broken pretzels
½ cup of peanuts
½ cup of cashews
2 tbsp. of peanut butter
Package of white chocolate chips
Package of peanut butter chips
Handful of chocolate chips
Cap of vanilla

Melt the all the chips together with the vanilla.
You can use the microwave or the stovetop.
When melted, mix in the peanut butter, peanuts,
cashews & pretzels.
Mix well!
Spread onto a greased 8x8 pan. I use cooking spray.
Let the fudge harden...about 2 hours.
Cut into chunks & enjoy.

99...100 Cookies!

1 cup of sugar
1 cup of brown sugar
1 cup of soft butter
1 cup of oil
1 egg
1 egg
Capful of vanilla
Pinch of salt
1 cup of chocolate chips (or more....I am a sucker for chocolate)
3 ½ cups of flour
1 tsp. of cream of tartar
1 tsp. of baking soda
1 cup of quick oats
1 cup of coconut
1 cup of chopped nuts
1 cup of krispie cereal

Mix all ingredients well.
Form the mixture into balls & place on cookie sheet.
Flatten slightly with the back of a spoon.
Bake 10-15 minutes at 350 degrees.
Cool & then stack.
Makes about 100 cookies...99 if you sample between baking.

Cow Patty Cappuccino

28 oz. of cocoa mix
1lb. of powdered sugar (about 3 ¾ cups)
8 qt. non-fat dry milk
16 oz. lite dairy creamer
8 oz. of instant coffee

Mix the ingredients.
Stir in an airtight container.
Use ¼ cup of mix to 1 cup of boiling water.
Sometimes I sprinkle in a few chocolate morsels for extra sweetness.

Quick Ass Root Beer

4 tsp. root beer extract
1 cup of water
1 ½ cups of sugar
1 tsp. dry yeast

Dissolve 1 teaspoon of dry yeast in 1 cup of warm water.
Pour that into a gallon jar or jug.
Add the sugar, root beer extract & warm water to mix
thoroughly until it's dissolved.
Add more water to the jar.
Set the jar in a warm place or in sunlight for several hours.
I usually make this in the morning & it is ready by lunch time.

What the Heck Crust Pumpkin Pie

1 cup of sugar
½ cup of flour
1 cup of pumpkin
½ cup of canned milk
4 eggs
Pinch of salt
1 tsp. of pumpkin pie spice
Whipped topping (optional)

Blend all the ingredients together well (except the whipped topping)
Pour the pie mixture into a sprayed or greased pan.
Bake at 350 degrees for 40 minutes.
When it's cooled...top with whipped cream.
Feel free to serve with ice cream!
YUMMY!

Cowboy Cody's Chocolate Buttermilk Sheet Cake

2 cups of sugar
2 cups of flour
Pinch of salt (about ¼ tsp. of salt)
1 tsp. of baking soda
3 T. of cocoa
½ cup of buttermilk
2 eggs
2 sticks of butter
Cap of vanilla
1 cup of water

FROSTING:
1 stick of butter
6 T. of milk
2 T. or more of cocoa
Cap of vanilla
1 lb. of powdered sugar
Chopped walnuts (optional)

Melt butter, cocoa, and water. Bring to a boil.
In a bowl mix sugar and flour together.
Add the butter, cocoa, and water mixture to the sugar and flour.
Add the eggs, buttermilk, salt, baking soda and vanilla.
Mix everything well.
Pour into greased (sprayed) sheet cake pan.
Bake at 350 degrees for 25 minutes.

For Frosting...melt butter, milk & cocoa.
Bring to a boil.
Pour over powdered sugar & beat until smooth.
Mix in vanilla & walnuts.

Polar Bear Snowman Candy

2 lbs. of almond bark
¼ cup of peanut butter
4 cups of krispies
1 cup of salted peanuts (or cashews…any nut of your choice)

Melt almond bark & peanut butter in microwave.
When that is melted add the krispies and nuts.
Drop on wax paper by teaspoon.
Let it cool.

Smart Ass Cake Doughnuts

4 egg yolks
1 cup of sugar
1 cup of milk
3 tbsp. of melted butter
Cap of vanilla
4 cups of flour
1 tsp. cream of tartar
1 tsp. of baking soda
Pinch of salt
1 tsp. of nutmeg
Mix the egg yolks, sugar, milk, butter and vanilla together.
Stir in the remaining ingredients (dry).
Roll out the dough.
Cut into doughnuts.
Put the doughnuts on waxed paper.
Let the doughnuts rise.
Fry in cooking oil.
Optional: roll in powdered sugar or granulated sugar.
ENJOY!

Make My Boobs Bigger Pie

1 ½ cups of milk
1 package of instant vanilla pudding
3 ½ cups of whipped cream
2 cups of chopped toffee bars
1 graham cracker crust
A cup or so of cherry pie filling (optional)

Mix milk & vanilla pudding together (whisk that bad boy together)
WHISK, WHISK, WHISK
Let it stand about one minute.

Stir in whipped topping, toffee and pie filling.
Pour into the crust and freeze it.
Remove from freezer about 10 minutes before serving your boob growing friends.

Witch Tit Peanut Butter Popcorn

Popped popcorn (I use about 10 cups)
½ to ¾ cup of honey
1/3 cup of sugar
½ cup of peanut butter (or more)
Cap of vanilla
½ cup of chocolate chips (optional)
Peanut Butter candies (optional)

Place the popcorn in a large bowl.
In a medium saucepan mix the honey, sugar, peanut butter, vanilla & chocolate chips over medium heat.
Pour the mixture over the popcorn.
Toss the popcorn a bit and then spread it onto a baking sheet.
Let it cool before serving it!
Enjoy!

The Beast Pumpkin Salad

1 can of pumpkin pie filling
1 (16 oz.) of whipped cream
Dash of pumpkin spice
Graham cracker crumbs

Mix pumpkin pie filling and whipped cream.
Add the pumpkin spice.
Top with graham cracker crumbs.
This can be a stand alone salad dish, or a side topping for ice cream.
It can even be used as a spread for pumpkin bread.

Cashew Cow Balls

42 caramels (unwrapped)
1 2/3 cup of cereal Krispies
1 cup of coconut (plus extra for rolling)
3 tbsp. of milk
1 cup (or a little more) of chopped cashews

In a microwave safe bowl, melt caramel & milk.
Stir
Add the Krispies, cup of coconut, and cashews.
Roll into balls and then into the extra coconut.
Put on waxed paper and covered container.
Freeze.

Big Texas Pudding

1 cup of flour
½ cup of sugar
2 tsp. of baking powder
½ tsp. of nutmeg
½ tsp. of cinnamon
Pinch of salt
1 tbsp. of butter (melted)
½ cup of milk
½ cup of raisins or dried cranberries
½ cup of brown sugar (set that aside)
2 cup of boiling water (set that aside)
Mix all the ingredients (except the brown sugar).
Pour into a casserole baking bowl that is sprayed/greased.
Sprinkle ½ cup of brown sugar over the top of the mixture.
Pour the 2 cups of water over everything.
Bake at 350 degrees for 60 minutes.
I serve this with ice cream...and some whipped topping.

Pumpkin Spice & Everything Nice Ice Cream

1 ½ cups of pumpkin
¾ cup of brown sugar
1 ½ quarts of vanilla ice cream (softened)
Graham crackers (crushed)
¾ tsp. of ginger
½ tsp. of nutmeg
¾ tsp. of cinnamon
Pinch of salt
Toffee candy bars crushed (optional)
Caramel sauce (optional)

Sprinkle crushed graham crackers on the bottom of a 9 x 13 pan.
Mix all the ingredients together (except the toffee candy bars)
Pour the mixture over the top of the graham crackers.
Sprinkle the top with toffee candy bars & caramel sauce.
Freeze!

S'more or Less

8 cups of cereal (I use Golden Grahams)
6 tbsp. of butter
6 cups of miniature marshmallows (divided up)
1/3 cup of light corn syrup
1 ½ cup of milk chocolate chips
Cap of vanilla
Crushed toffee candy bars (optional)
Melt 5 cups of marshmallows, corn syrup, butter, vanilla and chocolate chips over low heat.
Put the cereal in a large bowl.
Pour the stovetop mixture over the cereal.
Mix well.
Stir in the remaining marshmallows (1 cup)
Press mixture into a buttered/sprayed 9 x 13 pan.
Sprinkle crushed toffee candy on top.
Let is stand for at least an hour or put it in the refrigerator.
Yummy!

Truvy's Southern Belle Taffy

1 cup of sugar
1/3 cup of water
¼ cup of light corn syrup
1 T. of vinegar
¼ tsp. of baking soda
Butter (for your hands)

Mix sugar, water and syrup.
Stir over low heat until the sugar is dissolved.
Cook without stirring until the hard stage.
About 300 to 310 degrees.
Remove from heat.
Add vinegar & baking soda.
Stir until everything is mixed.
Pour into greased pan (I use a shallow one).
When it's cool enough to handle, butter your hands & pull the taffy until it turns white.
Pull into strips & cut into pieces.

Sheep Turd Droppings

1 T. butter or margarine
¼ cups of Karo syrup
2 squares of melted chocolate
Cap of vanilla
2 cups of powdered sugar
6 T. powered milk

Mix butter & syrup together.
Add the melted chocolate and blend well.
Add the vanilla, powdered sugar and dry milk.
Knead until the mixture is workable...make into shapes & chill.
Individually wrap them in plastic wrap.

Peanut Butter Pizza

 2 packages of refrigerated chocolate chip cookie dough (30 oz. total)
1 cup of creamy peanut butter
2 packages of regular marshmallows (20 oz. total)
1 cup of hot fudge sauce (I use more)
½ or more of salted peanuts or cashews
Crushed up candy bars (optional)

Slice the cookie dough into circular pieces and press it onto a large pizza pan.
Bake at 350 degrees for 10 minutes.
Remove from the oven.
Spread peanut butter on the pizza surface while it's still hot.
Cool.
Cover with marshmallows.
Bake at 400 degrees for 5 to 7 minutes.
Cook that until the marshmallows turn a light brown.
Remove from oven.
Drizzle with fudge sauce & sprinkle with cashews (or peanuts) and crushed up candy bars.

What are you waiting for....follow your dreams!

Horse Derby Pie

For crust:
Unbaked pie shell
1 cup of pecans (or nut of your choice)
1 cup of chocolate chips (I use a little more)

For Filling:
1 cup of sugar
½ cup of flour
Pinch of salt
1 stick of butter
Cap of vanilla
2 eggs (beaten)

In the unbaked pie shell, spread the pecans and chocolate chips on the bottom.

Beat the filling ingredients together.
Pour the filling mixture over the pie crust.
Bake at 350 degrees for 40 minutes.

Feel free to add more chocolate.

Blue Owl Sherbet

3 cups of milk
1 can of crushed pineapple
¾ cup of evaporated milk
1 pineapple juice concentrate, thawed (6 oz.)
1/3 cup of sugar
Cap of vanilla
Blue food coloring

Mix milk, pineapple (don't drain), evaporated milk, pineapple juice, sugar and vanilla.
Drop in food coloring. Use as much as you like.
Stir until well blended and the sugar dissolves.
Pour into a container.
Freeze!

Happier than a Camel on Wednesday Hot Fudge Pudding Cake

2 cups of flour
1 ½ cups of sugar
2 tsp. of baking powder
4 T of cocoa
Pinch of salt
1 cup of milk
½ cup of butter (melted)
2 caps of vanilla
Set aside: 2 cups of brown sugar & 6 or 7 tbsp. of cocoa

Mix all the pudding cake ingredients together.
Pour into a sprayed/greased 9 x 13 pan.

Next step:
Mix the 2 cups of brown sugar & cocoa together.

Spread the sugar & cocoa over the cake mixture in the pan.
Pour 3 ½ cups of VERY HOT WATER over the top.
DO NOT MIX
Bake for 40-45 minutes at 350 degrees.

The cake might take a moment to "set-up"...
I serve this warm with ice cream.

Pudgy's Peanut Butter Chocolate Cake

Cake ingredients:
2 cups of flour
2 cups of sugar
2/3 cup of cocoa
2 tsp. of baking soda
1 tsp. of baking powder
1 cup of brewed coffee (I use room temp. coffee)
Pinch of salt
2 eggs
1 cup of milk
2/3 cup of vegetable oil
Cap of vanilla
1 to 2 cups of chocolate chips—any kind (optional)

Place in a cake pan----bake for 30-35 minutes at 350 degrees.

Frosting ingredients:
3 oz. package of cream cheese
¼ cup of creamy peanut butter
2 cups of powdered sugar
2 tbsp. of milk
Cap of vanilla
Semi-sweet chocolate chips (optional)

Slap my Ass and Call Me Electa Cupcakes

Cupcake Ingredients:
2 ½ cups of flour
2 cups of sugar
5 T. of cocoa
Pinch of salt
3 tsp. of baking soda
2 eggs
Cap of vanilla
1 cup of HOT water
1 cup of vegetable oil
1 cup of buttermilk

Frosting:
1 stick of melted butter
1 lb. of powdered sugar
¼ cup of cocoa
1/3 cup of buttermilk
Cap of vanilla

Cupcakes: Mix all the ingredients together.
Bake in muffin tins at 350 degrees for 15 or so minutes.

Mix all the ingredients for frosting together.
Spread the frosting on the cupcakes when finished.

Not My First Rodeo Oatmeal Cake

Cake ingredients:
1 ¼ cups of water (boiling)
1 cup of oatmeal
½ cup of butter
1 cup of white sugar
1 cup of brown sugar
1 ½ cups of flour
2 eggs
Pinch of salt
Cap of vanilla
1 tsp. of cinnamon
1 tsp. of baking soda

Frosting:
5 tbsp. of brown sugar
3 tbsp. of butter
2 tbsp. of milk (maybe a little extra)
Powdered sugar
Coconut

Pour water over oatmeal and set aside.
Mix butter, white sugar, brown sugar, eggs, salt, vanilla, flour, cinnamon, and baking soda.
Add in the oatmeal.
Mix well.
Pour into a 9 x 13 pan.
Bake for 30 minutes.

Frosting:

Let the frosting mixture boil for one minute.

Remove from heat & slightly cool.

Add powdered sugar and coconut (you be the judge of how much to add)

Add a little milk if needed.

 Pour the frosting over the cake.

For added richness...when the cake is completely cooled, spread whipped topping to the top.

Sometimes I spread chocolate syrup or hot fudge sauce for extra kick.

Montana Moose Pies

4 cups of milk chocolate chips
1 cup of raisins
(although I use 1/2 cup of raisins & ½ cup of dried cranberries)
2 tbsp. of butter
1 cup of desired chopped nuts
(Almonds are typically used, but I like cashews)

On low heat melt butter & chocolate chips.
Remove from heat after the mixture is stirred.
Stir in raisins, dried cranberries & nuts.
Drop by spoonfuls onto waxed paper.
Chill!

Don't Eat Yellow Snow Lemon Bars...except these!

First step:
2 cups of flour
½ cup of powdered sugar
Pinch of salt
1 cup of butter
Cap of vanilla

Second step:
4 eggs
2 cups of sugar
5 or so tbsp. of lemon juice

Mix the first step ingredients together; flour, sugar, powdered sugar, salt, butter, & vanilla.
Press that bad boy mixture into the bottom of a 9 x 13 pan.
Bake for 15 to 20 minutes at 350 degrees.
Make the second step.
Mix the eggs, sugar & lemon juice together.
Remove the mixture from the oven.
Pour the filling over the top.
Bake for 25 minutes at 350 degrees.
When cool, sprinkle with powdered sugar.
Add a little whip cream, if needed.

Cowgirl Crazy Cobbler

1 stick of butter (melted)
1 cup of flour
1 cup of sugar
¾ cup of milk
1 ½ tsp. of baking powder
Cap of vanilla
Any fruit pie filling
Whipped topping (optional)

Put the melted butter into a 9 x 13 pan.
Mix vanilla, baking powder, milk, flour and sugar.
Pour that over the butter.
Pour pie filling over batter.
Bake at 350 degrees for 45 minutes.
Serve with whipped topping.

High Heels & Wearing Only an Apron Adult Mints

3 oz. of cream cheese
½ bag of powdered sugar
Flavoring of your choice (I use several drops)
Or I sometimes use peppermint schnapps alcohol
Lots of food coloring
Sugar (for mint molds)

Mix cream cheese & powdered sugar.
Knead that with hands.
Add flavoring and food coloring.
Sprinkle mint mold with white sugar.
Mold the mints.

Naked Hot Fudge Sauce

1 cup of sugar
¼ cup of cocoa
¼ flour
1 cup of water (boiling)
1 to 2 tbsp. of butter
1 teaspoon of grape jelly (optional)
Cap of vanilla
Tiny pinch of salt
If you would like to add a handful of milk chocolate chips…go for it!
Add sugar, cocoa, flour, & jelly to boiling water.
Boil until the sauce thickens.
Take off stove and add butter, vanilla, salt & chocolate chips.

Oh My God! Oatmeal Cut-Out Cookies

2 ½ cups of flour
1 cup of oatmeal
1 cup of butter
1 cup of sugar
1 egg
2 tbsp. of milk
Cap of vanilla
1 tsp. baking soda
Pinch of salt
Your favorite frosting

Mix all the ingredients together well (except the frosting)
Cover and chill for about 3 hours.
Heat oven to 350 degrees.
Roll out dough on floured surface.
Cut with a cookie cutter.
Bake for 8 to 10 minutes.
When cooled...frost with your favorite frosting & enjoy.

Hot Lava Applesauce

9 or 10 cooking apples
½ cup of water
½ cup of white sugar
½ cup of brown sugar
A few sprinkles of cinnamon

Peel, core & slice apples.
Put all the ingredients in a slow cooker.
Cover and cook on low for about 8 to 10 hours.
Or cook on high for 3 to 4 hours.
Serve with ice cream!

Magic Mitch's Pie

3 eggs
2/3 cup of sugar
1 cup of dark syrup
1 cup of pecans
1 tsp. of butter
Cap of vanilla
Pinch of salt
Handful of chocolate chips (optional)
One pie shell (unbaked)

Put pecans in the unbaked pie shell (9 inches).
Mix the other ingredients together.
Pour over the pecans.
Some pecans will rise to the top.
Bake at 350 degrees for 50 minutes.
Feel free to serve with ice cream.

Better Than Sex Cake

1 chocolate cake mix
1 cup of chocolate chips
1 can of sweetened condensed milk
1 jar of caramel topping
8 oz. of carton of whipped topping (thawed)
3 or so toffee candy bars (crushed)
Chocolate or caramel sauce (optional)

Mix the chocolate chips into the cake mix batter and bake according to the directions.
While the cake is still warm, poke holes in the baked cake. Pour the condensed milk all over the cake.
Cool it in the refrigerator. Later pour caramel over. Then top with whipped topping & crushed candy bars. I add chocolate & caramel sauce to the top of the cake. Store this in the refrigerator.
NOTE: You can heat and stir condensed milk & caramel sauce together and pour it over the cake.

Witty Kitty Hair Balls (Coconut Candy)

1 stick of butter (room temperature)
1 lb. of powdered sugar
2 (14 oz.) packages of coconut
1 can of evaporated milk
Favorite frosting (I use chocolate)

Mix butter, evaporated milk, powdered sugar and coconut together.
Mix well and spread mixture into pan.
Freeze for about an hour.
I spread frosting over the top....put it in the freezer a little longer.

Horse Tail Caramel Candy

½ lb. caramels
¼ cup of half & half (or ¼ cup of evaporated milk)
2 tbsp. of butter
2 cups of powdered sugar
17 or 18 of regular sized marshmallows
Food coloring (optional)

Mix caramels, half & half and butter in a saucepan.
Stir well.
Once everything is melted, take off the heat & gently stir in
powdered sugar.
In a 16 x 5 inch pan pour mixture onto buttered/sprayed wax
or parchment paper.
Lay the marshmallows end to end along one along one side
pan.
You can dot a little food coloring over the top, if you wish to
add a little color.
Detach the caramel from the paper & roll it over the
marshmallows to form a log.
Wrap the log in wax/parchment paper.
Refrigerate for a few hours.
When it's chilled, cut into about ½ inch slices.
Serve chilled.
I wrap these individually & store in an airtight container.
Place in the refrigerator.

French-Style Silk Pie

1 sm. Box of vanilla instant pudding
1 sm. Box of chocolate instant pudding
2 cups of milk
2 cups of vanilla (or chocolate) ice cream—softened
Whipped cream

Mix all the ingredients together, except the crust.
Pour the mixture into the crust.
Top with whipped cream.

Harness that Crazy Ass Attitude Apricot Bars

2 cups of sugar
2 cups of flour
1 cup of nuts (your choice)
1 tsp. of cinnamon
1 ½ tsp. of baking soda
2 jars of apricot baby food (or any flavor)
1 cup of oil
3 eggs
Pinch of salt
Cap of vanilla

Preheat oven to 350 degrees.
Mix all the ingredients together.
Beat until the batter is smooth.
Pour the mixture into a sprayed/greased cookie sheet.
Bake for 1 hour.
Remove from oven and sprinkle with powdered sugar.
Or you can put thin icing on top.

Cowgirl Up Gingersnaps

2 cups of flour
¾ cup of shortening
1 cup of sugar
1 egg
4 T. molasses
2 tsp. of baking soda
1 tsp. of cinnamon
1 tsp. of cloves
1 tsp. of ginger
Cap of vanilla

Mix all the ingredients together well.
Roll the dough into small balls.
Dip on side in sugar.
Place the balls on a cookie sheet, sugar side up.
Bake at 350 degrees for 10 to 15 minutes.

About the Author.....

Tipsy Tiffany believes in living life to the fullest.....having fun and no regrets! When she's not busy having a "girl's night", she's busy shopping, crafting, and trying new adventures. Be sure to check out Tipsy Tiffany at: www.tipsytiffany.com

Printed in Great Britain
by Amazon